The Surprising Power of Winning
One Day at a Time

THE 1-DAY METHOD

Antonio Neves

Copyright © 2025 by Antonio Neves

All rights reserved.

No portion of this book may be reproduced in any form without written permission from the publisher or author, except as permitted by U.S. copyright law.

Library of Congress Control Number: TXu002461797
Print ISBN: 979-8-218-61830-8

Published by THINQACTION Inc.

Book Cover Design and Interior Formatting by 100Covers.

Contents

Preface vii
Introduction ix

Chapter 1:   The Noise of More 1
Chapter 2:   The Seeds of Tomorrow 7
Chapter 3:   The Architecture of Today 13
Chapter 4:   The First Question 19
Chapter 5:   The Hours Before Dawn 25
Chapter 6:   When Less Becomes More 31
Chapter 7:   Five Acts of Living 37
Chapter 8:   The Eternal Today 45
Chapter 9:   In Sacred Company 53
Chapter 10: The Day That Changes
                Everything 59

Epilogue: Your Journey Begins 67
About The 1 Day Method™ 71
About The Author 73

For Gigi, August, & Harper
We are the Neves family.

Preface

Life has a way of stripping everything down to what matters.

In 2025, wildfires took everything from my family. Our home. Our belongings. Our safety.

When you lose everything, you learn something profound: Life doesn't wait.

It moves in days.
In choices.
In moments.

As I write these words, I'm using The 1-Day Method™ to rebuild our life from scratch. Not tomorrow. Now.

This method isn't theory.

It's how you move forward when
moving forward feels impossible.

The truth is, we're all rebuilding something.

This book isn't about what was lost.
It's about what we choose to build today.

Let's begin.

Introduction

Most lives are lost in the space between intention and action. In the gap between someday's promise and today's reality. In the quiet surrender of now for later.

But life whispers a truth few are ready to hear:
Your days are not stepping stones to your life
They are your life
Each sunrise to sunset
Complete in itself
Perfect in its possibility

The 1 Day Method™ isn't another system promising future transformation. It's a return to what your soul already knows:

Today is all you have. Today is all you need.

For over a decade, I've watched the pattern:
Brilliant minds scattered across
tomorrow's dreams
Powerful spirits trapped in someday's plans
Endless potential waiting for
the perfect moment

But those who transformed
understood something simple:
Life moves in days
Power lives in presence
Change happens now, or not at all

Who This Book Is For

This book speaks to those who feel the gap:
Between their potential and their reality
Between their intentions and their actions
Between who they are and who they could be

The 1-Day Method

It's for the ambitious who've grown tired of:
Endless productivity hacks that
complicate the simple
Five year plans that ignore today's power
Digital solutions that fragment attention
Morning routines that feel
like another obligation

This is for:
The entrepreneur whose vision
exceeds their current reality
The professional whose impact
is diluted by daily chaos
The parent balancing big dreams
with present demands
The achiever whose scattered
focus is stealing their power

If you sense that your life's noise
is drowning its music,
If you feel the weight of unreached potential,

If you know there's more but
can't find your way there…
You're in the right place.

But know this:
This book won't coddle you with complexity
Won't distract you with tools
Won't promise overnight transformation

Instead, it offers something rarer:
A return to power through presence
A path to growth through simplicity
A way forward through today

What You'll Learn

What follows isn't another compilation
of strategies and systems.
It's a stripping away
Of complexity that clouds wisdom
Of noise that drowns truth
Of future thinking that steals present power

The 1-Day Method

Each chapter returns you to simplicity
To clarity
To the surprising power of a
single day fully lived

The final chapter doesn't add. It completes
Doesn't complicate. It clarifies
Doesn't promise. It reveals

Remember:
Your future isn't coming
It's growing
From this moment
This choice
This day

The journey begins now.

Chapter 1

The Noise of More

Life speaks in whispers, but we live in shouts. In endless notifications. In countless apps promising optimization. In systems meant to make us better, faster, stronger.

Most spend their lives drowning in solutions to problems they never had. They mistake complexity for advancement. Activity for achievement. Noise for wisdom.

The truth is simpler, but harder to hear.

The Promise of Systems

Watch how the modern world operates: Selling complexity as salvation

Trading peace for productivity
Promising "more" as the path to meaning

Every notification a small theft of presence
Every app another fragment of attention
Every system another layer
between you and truth

The tools meant to free you
became your prison.

The Seduction of More

Society runs on a simple deception:
More goals will make you better
More tracking will make you stronger
More apps will make you wiser

But wisdom flows the other way:
Through subtraction, not addition
Through focus, not fragmentation
Through presence, not productivity

The Five Year Illusion

"Where do you see yourself in five years?"

This question has derailed more lives than failure ever could. It forces artificial timelines on organic growth. It demands certainty in an uncertain world.

Life doesn't move in five year plans.
It moves in moments.
In choices.
In days.

The Currency of Attention

Your attention isn't just yours anymore:
It's claimed by notifications
Divided by devices
Scattered by systems

But power lives in protection:
Of your time
Of your focus
Of your presence

The Way Forward

Progress isn't found in more goals,
more apps, or more promises.
It's found in:
- Moments fully lived
- Priorities clearly chosen
- Days intentionally designed

The solution isn't to stop dreaming.
It's to start living.
Hour by hour.
Day by day.
Choice by choice.

Key Insights
- Complexity obscures wisdom
- Systems don't equal solutions
- Protection beats productivity
- Presence outperforms planning
- Simple truths create profound change

The rest of this book will show you a different path. Not through more complexity, but through returned simplicity. Not through better systems, but through deeper wisdom.

Truth awaits in silence.

Chapter 2

The Seeds of Tomorrow

Time reveals its secrets slowly. In choices that seem small. In habits that whisper their consequences. In days that stack silently into destinies.

Most live caught between two illusions: that yesterday determines their future, or that tomorrow holds their change. They miss the profound power of now.

The Mathematics of Moments

Watch closely how life unfolds:
Not in dramatic leaps
Not in sudden transformations
Not in tomorrow's promises

But in today's quiet choices:
A moment of movement or comfort
A decision to create or consume
A choice to grow or repeat

Your future isn't a mystery.
It's a reflection of now.

The Control Paradox

Life offers less control than we imagine, yet more than we use.

You can't control:
The market's movement
Other's choices
Time's passage

But you always control:
Your next response
Your present focus
Your immediate choice

This isn't about perfection.
It's about presence.

Lead and Lag

Most chase shadows:
Numbers on scales
Figures in accounts
Titles on walls

These are lag measures.
Echoes of past choices.

But wisdom lives in lead measures:
Today's small choice
This hour's focus
This moment's decision

The Scorecard of Now

Life keeps perfect accounts:
Each choice adding or subtracting

Each moment investing or spending
Each day building or eroding

Not in dramatic sums
But in quiet additions:
A page read
A conversation had
A promise kept

The Seeds You Plant

Every moment plants something:
Either weeds of distraction
Or seeds of intention

Every hour grows something:
Either walls of resistance
Or paths of possibility

Every day builds something:
Either caves of comfort
Or bridges to growth

Key Insights
- Present choices whisper future realities
- Control lives in immediate responses
- Lead measures shape lag measures
- Small actions compound silently
- Today's seeds become tomorrow's forest

Tomorrow isn't coming.
It's growing.
From this moment.
This choice.
This day.

Tend your garden wisely.

Chapter 3

The Architecture of Today

Every civilization has understood a truth we've forgotten: Life doesn't unfold in grand sweeps of destiny. It unfolds in sunrises and sunsets. In mornings and evenings. In todays.

Most chase horizons, believing life awaits somewhere ahead. They store their power in distant goals, not realizing that tomorrow is built in the quiet architecture of today.

The Nature of Time

Watch how time actually moves:
Not in years that loom
Not in months that stretch
Not in weeks that blur

But in days:
Clear as sunrise
Complete as sunset
Perfect in their bounds

The Present's Power

Life offers a peculiar truth:
Yesterday is just memory
Tomorrow is just dream
Only today holds reality

This isn't philosophy.
It's physics.
Is-ness versus might-be.
Reality versus illusion.

The Chess Master's Secret

Study those who achieve mastery:
They don't obsess over tournaments ahead

They don't dwell on matches past
They focus on the move before them

Excellence isn't built in someday
It's built in this moment
This choice
This day

The Foundation Formula

Watch how real change happens:
Not through future fantasies
But through present practices
Not through distant dreams
But through daily decisions

Each day a complete universe
Each moment a fresh chance
Each choice a new beginning

The Quiet Victory

Success leaves breadcrumbs:
Not in grand gestures
But in small completions
Not in perfect plans
But in present actions

Today's small win
Becomes tomorrow's strength
Becomes next week's momentum
Becomes life's direction

The Power of Now

Here's what separates wisdom from wishes:
- Wisdom lives in today
- Wisdom works with what is
- Wisdom builds through presence

Key Insights

- Days are life's true currency
- Present power beats future potential
- Small actions compound silently
- Today's choices shape tomorrow's reality
- Now is where transformation lives

Your day awaits.
Not to be conquered.
But to be lived.
Fully.
Completely.
Presently.

This moment holds everything.

Chapter 4

---✱---

The First Question

Life moves in questions, not answers. The most important question isn't what you'll achieve, but what will make this day matter.

Most lives are lost in the first hour of consciousness. A glance at a screen. A scroll through demands. The surrender of intention to inbox.

The quiet truth is this: Your day belongs to whoever claims it first.

The Power of Definition

Watch closely and you'll see two types of lives:
Those defined by circumstance.
Those defined by intention.

The difference isn't in their capabilities.
It's in their first conscious choice.

Before the world can hand you its
agenda, you must know your own.
Before others can steal your attention,
you must know what deserves it.

The question waits: What will
make today matter?

The Architecture of Meaning

Success without definition is motion
without meaning. Energy without
direction. Time without purpose.

Yet look at how most approach their days:
Email determines their priorities
Notifications shape their focus
Others' urgency becomes their compass

They drift in the currents of external demands,
wondering why they never reach their shore.

The Nature of Time

Time teaches us something subtle:
What you react to owns you.
What you define frees you.

Most people live at the mercy of
what demands attention.
Few live by what deserves attention.

The difference lies in three things:
What you decide matters
What you choose to protect
What you dare to celebrate

Everything else is noise.

The Morning Contract

Each sunrise offers the same invitation:
To define your day before the
world defines it for you
To choose your priorities before
chaos chooses them
To protect what matters before life dilutes it
To prepare for victory before
business drowns it

This isn't about perfection.
It's about intention.
About clarity.
About freedom.

Key Insights
- Your day belongs to who claims it first
- Definition precedes direction
- Intention beats reaction
- Clarity creates freedom
- Today's meaning is tomorrow's momentum

Your day awaits its definition.
The question remains:
What will make it matter?

The answer changes everything.

Chapter 5

The Hours Before Dawn

There's a particular kind of silence
in the early hours. A clarity that
visits before the world wakes.

Most seek more time by stretching their
days longer. By adding hours at the
edges. By stealing from their rest.

But time isn't found in extension.
It's found in silence.
In the hours before dawn.

The Quality of Hours

All hours carry time.
Few carry possibility.

Watch those who seem to bend time
to their will. They don't work more
hours. They own better ones.

The hours before sunrise hold a
different kind of currency:
Silence instead of noise
Creation instead of reaction
Possibility instead of demand

The Evening's Promise

A profound truth hides in plain sight:
Great mornings are born in the evening.

Most chase the sunrise with willpower.
Few understand that dawn's
victory is won at dusk.

Your evening choices whisper to your morning:
The screen that steals your rest

The food that fights your sleep
The habits that hollow your energy

Tomorrow's power lies in tonight's decisions.

The Sanctuary of Sleep

Your bedroom tells the truth about
your relationship with time.
It's either serving your awakening
or securing your slumber.

Sleep isn't surrender.
Rest isn't retreat.
They're investments in clarity.

Make your room a temple of renewal:
Darkness to honor your rhythms
Silence to restore your mind
Distance from the world's demands

The Dawn Decision

Each evening presents life's most honest trade:
Comfort now or clarity later
Distraction now or direction later
Entertainment now or energy later

This isn't about deprivation.
It's about priorities.
About possibilities.
About power.

The Compound Effect

Consider what shifts when you
claim the early hours:
Clarity before confusion sets in
Direction before demands arise
Movement before the world moves you

This isn't just about time.
It's about sovereignty.
Over your hours.
Over your energy.
Over your life.

Key Insights
- Dawn's silence carries unique power
- Evening choices create morning freedom
- Sleep is an investment, not an expense
- Early hours compound differently
- Sovereignty starts in silence

The early hours aren't waiting to be filled.
They're waiting to be claimed.

Silence beckons.

Chapter 6

When Less Becomes More

A peculiar truth reveals itself when you study those who move mountains: Their power doesn't come from doing more, but from doing less with complete presence.

Most chase expansion. More goals. More tasks. More commitments. They spread themselves across life like water on concrete. A millimeter deep but covering everything.

The wisest among us know better.
They understand that power rises
from reduction, not addition.

The Physics of Focus

Your mind carries infinite
possibility but finite energy.
Every open loop drains it.
Every competing priority splits it.
Every unnecessary commitment weakens it.

This isn't philosophy.
It's physics.

The Rule of Three

Life whispers a truth few are
quiet enough to hear:
If you have more than three
priorities, you have none.

Watch how most minds operate:
Lists that never end
Attention that never settles
Energy that never concentrates

They mistake movement for progress.
Busy for purposeful.
Many for meaningful.

The Art of Selection

Each morning offers a moment
of profound power:
The chance to choose your essential three.

Not what screams loudest.
Not what seems urgent.
Not what others demand.

But what moves the deepest
currents of your life.

The Question of Impact

The wise choose by asking:
What will matter beyond today?
What serves my deepest truth?

What builds tomorrow's foundation?

Everything else is secondary.
Everything else can wait.
Everything else is noise.

The Morning's Invitation

Before the world hands you
its agenda, you choose:
One priority that shapes your future
One that strengthens your present
One that honors your path

Three.
Clear.
Protected.

The Freedom of Bounds

Something shifts when you embrace three:
Clarity replaces confusion

Focus defeats distraction
Depth overcomes shallow

This isn't about ignoring life's complexity.
It's about honoring life's essence.

The Essential Truth

Each sunrise asks quietly:
What three actions will echo beyond today?

Not what you should do.
Not what you could do.
But what will matter when the noise fades.

Key Insights
- Power lives in reduction
- Focus follows elimination
- Three priorities create more progress than ten
- Selection beats addition
- Depth requires bounds

Your essential three await their selection.
Choose with care.
Protect with vigor.
Honor with action.

Simplicity illuminates the path.

Chapter 7

Five Acts of Living

In the quietest moments of dawn, life reveals its deepest pattern: Transformation isn't found in monumental achievements. It lives in small acts done with infinite presence.

Most chase significance in spectacle. In summits reached. In milestones marked. In destinations claimed. They miss the sacred hiding in plain sight, in five acts that, done with presence, change everything.

The First Act: Return to Body

Your body holds wisdom older than thought:
Deeper than strategy
Ancient as breath
Pure as presence

Movement isn't exercise
It's remembrance
Of what you were before words
Of what you are beneath names
Of power that precedes thinking

Twenty minutes of pure motion does
more than strengthen muscle:
It awakens cellular memory
It clears the mind's ancient shadows
It returns you to original truth
It reminds you of who you were before
the world told you who to be

The Second Act: True Connection

In an age where touch has become digital
Where presence has become pixels
Where connection has become clicks
Something ancient calls us back

Not to messages sent
Not to information shared
But to the sacred space between two humans
Where souls meet without screens
Where truth transfers without words
Where power multiplies through presence

This isn't networking
It's remembering we are not
alone in the universe
It's returning to our first language
The one spoken before words

The Third Act: Eternal Growth

Life presents a daily invitation:
Not to acquire knowledge
But to become more fully yourself

Growth isn't measured in achievements:
But in questions that open doors
In insights that arrive like old friends

In wisdom that feels like remembering
In truth that changes everything

This isn't about adding
It's about unveiling
Not about gaining
But becoming

The Fourth Act: Sacred Silence

Technology promised connection
Instead, it fragmented our essence
Scattered our presence
Divided our power

But in ten minutes of pure silence
Lives more wisdom than ten hours of noise
More power than ten days of action
More truth than ten years of searching

Silence isn't emptiness
It's fullness
It's not absence
It's essence

The Fifth Act: The Joy of Completion

Each day asks for one complete thing:
Not a step toward tomorrow
Not a promise about someday
But something honored into wholeness

Completion isn't about checking boxes
It's about closing circles
About honoring beginnings with endings
About bringing something into being
About keeping promises to yourself

The Integration

These aren't tasks to rush through
They're invitations to full living:

Sweat - Return to original wisdom
Connect - Remember your humanity
Grow - Stay eternally curious
Tech Free - Find your center
Finish - Honor your word

Key Insights
- Movement awakens ancient knowing
- True connection heals modern fragments
- Growth happens in quiet openings
- Silence reveals what noise conceals
- Completion builds trust with the universe

The 1-Day Method

Five simple acts
Done with presence
Changed by intention
Transformed by attention

Life waits in the ordinary
Power lives in pattern
Truth hides in simplicity
Change happens in presence

Your five acts await.

Chapter 8

The Eternal Today

In the ancient wisdom traditions, they speak of satori. Moments of perfect clarity when time stops being a river and becomes an ocean. When future and past dissolve into the perfect wholeness of now.

Most lives scatter across time's illusion. They store their power in tomorrow's vault, their excuses in yesterday's archives. They treat today as a bridge to cross rather than a temple to enter.

The Nature of Now

Watch how life actually moves:
Not in planned tomorrows
Not in remembered yesterdays

But in this breath
This heartbeat
This infinite moment

Each sunrise whispers the same truth:
This day isn't preparation for your life
It is your life
Complete in its incompleteness
Perfect in its imperfection
Whole in its becoming

The Architecture of Presence

Life builds itself like a coral reef:
Not through grand design
But through countless small accumulations
Each moment a tiny crystal
Each choice a new branch
Each day a complete universe

Watch how true growth happens:
Not through declarations of future glory
Not through promises of distant triumph
But through moments fully claimed
Through breaths fully taken
Through choices fully owned

The Witness Within

Success leaves traces more
subtle than footprints:
Not in spectacular moments
Not in pinnacle achievements
But in quiet acknowledgments
In small victories witnessed
In subtle shifts honored
In presence recognized

Each win becomes evidence
Not of what you'll do
But of who you're becoming

Not of where you'll arrive
But of who you are in this moment

The Evening's Contemplation

As light fades, wisdom asks:
Not what did you achieve
Not what did you acquire
But what mattered?
What moved?
What deserves witness?
What truth emerged?

This isn't about keeping score
It's about keeping faith
With yourself
With your path
With the eternal now

The Alchemy of Today

Notice how life actually unfolds:
Today's clarity feeds tomorrow's vision
Today's choice shapes tomorrow's options
Today's presence creates tomorrow's power

This isn't motivation
This is physics
Simple
Eternal
True

The Nature of Setbacks

Some days won't feel like victories
This is natural
This is human
This is life

But even in apparent failure
Lives tomorrow's wisdom
Waits tomorrow's strength
Grows tomorrow's understanding
Blooms tomorrow's grace

The Present's Promise

Here's what separates wisdom from wishing:
Wisdom lives only in now
Wisdom builds through acknowledgment
Wisdom grows through presence
Wisdom flows through acceptance

Key Insights
- Now holds all the power you'll ever need
- Small shifts create profound change
- Witnessed progress builds unstoppable momentum
- Present choices shape future possibilities
- Each day offers its own completion

The 1-Day Method

This moment asks nothing of you
Except presence
Except acknowledgment
Except truth
Except now

The eternal today awaits its witness.

Chapter 9

In Sacred Company

In the deepest mysteries of existence lies a beautiful paradox: Your most profound individuality flourishes only in the soil of connection. Your unique path reveals itself most clearly in the light of shared wisdom.

Most guard their growth like a secret, wearing independence as armor. They mistake solitude for strength, not seeing that even the mightiest redwoods share nutrients beneath the soil, their roots dancing in eternal conversation.

The Pattern of Connection

Watch how wisdom actually moves:
Not in isolation
But in resonance

Not in private revelation
But in shared illumination
Not in solo victories
But in collective celebration

When souls gather in purpose:
One truth becomes many
One insight ignites others
One victory feeds thousands
One day's power multiplies

The Mirror of Souls

Your reflection lives beyond your eyes:
In those who see your unfolding
In those who hold your becoming
In those who witness your daily truth
In those who understand your sacred journey

This isn't about dependency
It's about resonance

About reflection
About the multiplication of presence
About the amplification of power

The Alchemy of Together

Something profound happens
when presence multiplies:
Intention finds its mirror
Purpose finds its echo
Truth finds its witness
Power finds its amplification

Watch how real transformation flows:
Someone rises before dawn beside you
Someone moves toward truth with you
Someone holds space for your becoming
Someone celebrates your daily victories

Together, days gather new power:
Intentions find their garden

Habits find their soil
Victories find their chorus
Truth finds its temple

The Sacred Tools

Even simple objects carry collective wisdom:
A book holds ancestral knowing
A journal carries gathered truth
A planner contains distilled presence

But these are just the beginning
They open doors to deeper communion
To shared journeys
To collective rising
To multiplied power

The Symphony of Being

True transformation has its own music:
The rhythm of shared intention

The harmony of mutual presence
The melody of collective celebration
The symphony of unified purpose

This isn't about losing yourself in others
It's about finding yourself through others
In sacred company
In shared presence
In collective wisdom

Key Insights
- No profound truth walks alone
- Real strength flows through connection
- Individual power multiplies in communion
- Support transforms possibility into reality
- Together carries more wisdom than alone

Your journey seeks its witnesses
Your growth seeks its garden
Your truth seeks its chorus
Your power seeks its multiplication

Find your sacred circle
Join your soul's tribe
Share your inner light
Multiply your presence

The communion awaits.

Chapter 10

The Day That Changes Everything

In the end, all wisdom circles back to a single, luminous truth: Life doesn't unfold in the grand sweep of years or in the distant horizons of someday. It reveals itself in the sacred territory of today, in the eternal dance between sunrise and sunset.

The 1 Day Method™ isn't another system attempting to tame time. It's a return to what your soul has always known: Today isn't a step toward your life. It is your life, complete in its becoming, perfect in its possibility.

The Dawn's Remembrance

Most begin their days in
unconscious surrender:
To screens that fragment essence
To demands that scatter presence
To noise that drowns wisdom
To future that steals now

But dawn offers ancient remembrance:
Silence before clamor
Intention before reaction
Presence before performance
Being before doing

The Sacred Question

Before the world hands you its agenda,
something deeper whispers:
Not what should be done

Not what could be done
But what deserves your precious presence?
What calls to your deepest truth?
What moves your eternal becoming?

This isn't about productivity
It's about presence
About essence
About the sacred dance between
What is and what could be

The Power of Three

Life reveals its deepest magic in limitation:
Three priorities
Clear as mountain streams
Protected as sacred ground
Perfect in their simplicity

Everything else is beautiful, but secondary
Everything else is worthy, but waiting
Everything else is possible, but not now
Everything else dims in the
light of essential truth

The Five Acts of Being

Each day invites five sacred practices:

Sweat - Remember your original strength
Not just movement
But communion with life's flow
But return to body's wisdom
But dance with ancient knowing

Connect - Touch eternal truth
Not just conversation
But soul meeting soul
But heart touching heart
But presence multiplying presence

Grow - Honor endless unfolding
Not just learning
But becoming
But unfolding
But remembering who you've always been

Tech Free - Return to silence
Not just disconnection
But reunion with essence
But communion with source
But return to original silence

Finish - Complete the circle
Not just doing
But bringing something into being
But honoring intention with completion
But closing sacred circles

The Evening's Contemplation

As light fades, wisdom whispers:
What mattered?

What moved?
What deserves witness?
What truth emerged?
What beauty unfolded?

Record your victories
Not to measure
But to remember
Not to prove
But to honor
Not to track
But to celebrate

The Method's Essence

This path works because it
honors life's deepest truth:
- Every day is a complete journey
- Every moment holds perfect power
- Every choice shapes eternal now

- Every act builds tomorrow's foundation
- Every acknowledgment feeds future strength

The journey never starts tomorrow
It doesn't await perfect conditions
It lives in this breath
This choice
This moment
This sacred now

Key Insights
- Dawn carries ancient power
- Clear intention shapes reality
- Three priorities hold sacred focus
- Five acts transform ordinary into eternal
- Witnessed victories feed the soul's journey

This isn't merely method
It's remembrance
Of what you've always known

Of who you've always been
Of what's always been true
Of where power truly lives

Today awaits its witness
Now awaits its recognition
Life awaits your presence
Power awaits your claim

The eternal moment is here.

Epilogue

Your Journey Begins

Life offers a beautiful and sometimes
harsh truth: No one owes you anything,
but you owe yourself everything.

Think about that for a moment.
Your dreams don't care about your excuses.
Your potential doesn't accept your reasons.
Your future isn't waiting for perfect conditions.

People will support you. They'll cheer
for you. They'll celebrate your victories.
But no one, absolutely no one, can care
about your life more than you do.

This is both burden and gift:
Burden because there's nowhere to hide
Gift because there's nothing holding you back

The path forward is remarkably simple:
Win today.
Then win tomorrow.
Then win the next day.

When confusion comes. Win today.
When doubt creeps in. Win today.
When motivation fades. Win today.

You don't need to see the whole staircase.
You don't need to know every turn in the road.
You just need to know what
makes today matter.

To support you on this journey, we've
created The 1 Day Method™ Planner.
Not another digital distraction, but a
physical companion. A daily reminder
of what matters. A sacred space for your
intentions, your priorities, your victories.

The 1-Day Method

But whether you use our planner or
find another way, remember this:
Your life moves in days
Your power lives in now
Your future builds through presence

The world will try to complicate this truth.
It will try to sell you complexity.
It will try to make you doubt your power.

Don't let it.

The simple truth remains:
A great life starts with a great day.
A great day starts with clear intention.
Clear intention starts with you.

Your journey begins now.
Not tomorrow.
Not someday.
Now.

Win today.

The rest will follow.

The1DayMethod.com

About The 1 Day Method™

The 1 Day Method™ transforms how people approach life, work, and personal growth. Beyond this book, it encompasses:

The 1 Day Method™ Planner: Your daily companion for winning each day
Speaking & Workshops: Taking the method deeper
Online Resources: Supporting your journey

Thousands have used this method to create extraordinary lives through simple, powerful daily practices.

To learn more about The 1 Day Method™ and join our community:

Visit: www.the1daymethod.com

About The Author

Antonio Neves believes that life's deepest transformations happen in the space between sunrises. Not in grand plans, but in days fully lived.

The creator of The 1 Day Method™, Antonio is a bestselling author, international keynote speaker, and award-winning journalist whose work has reached millions through NBC, PBS, MTV Networks, and the NBC TODAY Show. His previous book, *Stop Living on Autopilot*, helped countless readers across the globe reclaim their power and purpose.

As a former NCAA athlete and Ivy League graduate, Antonio learned early that daily choices shape destinies. Now, as a leadership expert, husband, and father of two, he shares this wisdom with organizations and individuals worldwide, proving that extraordinary lives are built one intentional day at a time.

Based in Los Angeles, Antonio continues to explore the intersection of daily practice and lasting transformation, helping others discover that their best life isn't waiting in some distant future, it's waiting in how they spend today.

TheAntonioNeves.com
@TheAntonioNeves

www.ingramcontent.com/pod-product-compliance
Lightning Source LLC
LaVergne TN
LVHW020937090426
835512LV00020B/3404